day/break

day/break

Gwen Benaway

Book*hug Press
Toronto 2020

LIBRARY AND ARCHIVES CANADA CATALOGUING IN PUBLICATION

Title: Day/break / Gwen Benaway.
Other titles: Daybreak
Names: Benaway, Gwen, 1987– author.
Description: Poems
Identifiers: Canadiana (print) 20200158929 | Canadiana (ebook) 20200158988
ISBN 9781771665735 (softcover) | ISBN 9781771665742 (HTML)
ISBN 9781771665759 (PDF) | ISBN 9781771665766 (Kindle)
Classification: LCC PS8603.E5561 D39 2020 | DDC C811/.6—dc23

PRINTED IN CANADA

The production of this book was made possible through the generous assistance
of the Canada Council for the Arts and the Ontario Arts Council. Book*hug
Press also acknowledges the support of the Government of Canada through
the Canada Book Fund and the Government of Ontario through the
Ontario Book Publishing Tax Credit and the Ontario Book Fund.

Book*hug Press acknowledges that the land on which we operate is the
traditional territory of many nations, including the Mississaugas of the Credit,
the Anishnabeg, the Chippewa, the Haudenosaunee and the Wendat peoples.
We recognize the enduring presence of many diverse First Nations, Inuit
and Métis peoples and are grateful for the opportunity to meet and
work on this territory.

Cover photo by Filip Mroz (via Unsplash)
Interior cover photo by Syed Ahmed (via Unsplash)

"If I'm transformed by language, I am often
crouched in footnote or blazing in title.
Where in the body do I begin."

—Layli Long Soldier, *Whereas*

trans women are objects we must perform the gender
of our bodies beaten to death by men in viral videos on
Facebook a crowd mocks a trans woman in Paris then
chases her down a street before punching her a man stabs
his trans girlfriend more than forty times in the front seat
of his car in a parking lot at 2 am my best friend texts me
that she wants to die and I and I and I and I and and I

don't know how to stay alive

I refuse I refuse I refuse I refuse I make light I refuse I
refuse I refuse I offer up my body I refuse I refuse I refuse
I refuse I live I refuse I refuse I refuse I refuse I imagine
elsewhere I refuse I refuse I refuse I refuse I refuse I
withhold I refuse I refuse I refuse I refuse I refuse I persist
I refuse I reuse I refuse
                            I
        am not
                        an object
I inscribe my gender like a bruise on the perfect smooth flesh of
        your bright morning
                    the dawn (and I)
    begin as colour across the horizon, granulated and coarse, not
                ordered or linear, submerged in light and dark
                        incorrigible diffuse daybreak
I confess my beauty

                        then you murder it.

1

I am not a girl
but a creature made of smoke
and exhaustion.

                    I want a poem scrubbed of
                    dignity,
                              a body
                                      not brave
                              but present.

          once
after fucking me hard
in a bedroom filled with dust,

you said I was more or less
like a biological woman.

                    I carry your words inside my body
                              like the night carries the moon—

              each time I wake,
                  less of me is left.

                still, the low sounds
                of the city rise up
                to wash my hands clean
                of longing

              my morning cigarette
                  is a prayer
                              to mourn
                              the end of sleep.

            look to your own horizon

tell me what you see.

                    is it my breasts,
                    wet with your saliva,
                    returning to press
                    against memory

or does nothing of me remain?

           I asked for this, didn't I?

      to be in love
         and not broken,

        luminous,
             suspended in air.

brief light
          of this new day,

                  bless us
                  in our forgetting.

a tranny is a girl
who sold her dignity
        for a chance
        to be human.

                I am the lesser woman,
                        transformed by scalpel
                        and the indifference of men.

        their careful pity
        marks my body,
                the border
                between want
                                and shame.

call me hunger
        and place your flesh
        on my lips.

                        I want a gender
                            that does more
                            than perform apology.

        I break bread
        on the shoreline
                and offer my throat
                to the crows.

dip your hands

        in my wet
                and dive, lover.

I'm here,
a mistake
as much as envy.

3

the summer we met
        I was 5'7 and 130 pounds,

all thirst and hunger but rail thin,
        my hip bones jutting
            out of pale skin.

you poured me over
        your body,

            musk stung
              and glistening.

before you,
        I knew nothing of how deep
        abjection

            could wound me.

now I've layered fat over
        the places you touched
      and held my fingers
        against my labia

as if pressing a knife cut
    shut.

        please say my name
        between the hours of dawn
        and nightfall.

each consonant
        will be a moth

in flight, circling
what light lingers.

rape is such
a small word
to hold what passed
between you and me.

I want you
to remember

that summer heat,
the roiling night clouds,
hum of insect and passerby,

my mouth
against your neck,

the dull wet sound
my body made
beneath you.

4

a poem
 or a transsexual is never

 made or unmade

 by our descriptions,

 the chromosomal
 line breaks.

I would rather be a trick of metaphor
 than a phantom of everyday failure.

 how my body
 conjures the ugly ruined world,

 my blemished skin,
 imperfect pitch.

 there's a limit
 to language—

 each morning
 the sun sweeps across the glass
 towers in my city,
 breaks into a million vessels
 of flicker and blaze.

 no one talks about
 the ordinary wonder
 of daybreak
 though we wait for its arrival.

it's the same with a woman
or a girl—
not worth praising,
beyond words.

this is what the poem
and a transsexual want,

to be past
what can never be said
in proper speech,

to remain,
inviolate and brazen,

in the margins
of the sky.

5

I remember the weight
　　of your arm
　　slung over my shoulders
　　as we walked down
　　Yonge Street.

　　　　the yoke of your body,
　　　　　　how you parted seas of people
　　　　　　and muddied light to pull me

　　　　　　　　　behind you.

　　　　loving a white man is

　　　　　　to be a passenger
　　　　　　in the wake
　　　　　　　　of his wanting.

6

did I ever tell you about the other boy?

I must have.

he was your opposite,

    gentle and withdrawn,
    refused to touch me
        with anything
        but grace.

            his body
            came between us
               in conversation,

          I wanted your jealousy to rise
          and drown me.

          I never gave him a chance
          to love me,

        determined
          to have your hate
          fill me full

           of oceanic sediment.

I let him kiss me
    in a rented car
        in scarborough,
            his hands of night
               and aftershave.

how much I failed

                 by not imagining more
                 from love,

        accepting someone's fetish
        as my price,

playing queer in the absence
    of any other name for what it means
    to fuck a girl
    like me.

to write of wanting,
>>to say "trans,"
>>meaning more
>>>>than identity,

>>>>lay claim
>>>>to this body
>>>>>>of pleasure
>>>>>>and skyline,

>>to be undone
>>>>by the scent of tree pollen
>>>>in a man's hair,
>>>>>>how the damp skin
>>>>>>of his lower back
>>>>>>>>could be a field
>>>>>>>>of yellow hay,

>>to admit failure,
>>>>the imperfect lust
>>>>>>of a woman
>>>>>>>>with no right
>>>>>>>>to call herself
>>>>>>>>>>female.

to linger in the shallows of love,
>>>>its oxbow curve
>>>>>>and glacial drainage,

>>>>to be sentimental
>>>>without justification,

praise the hymns
of city noon,
        make elegies of
        fast-food wrappers,

                to conjure stretch marks
                    and body hair,

           bear the weight of too much wanting
                without the defence of beauty

                        or hope.

8

why remember
    the tiny details,

        your Minnesota accent,
        your brown beard
            against my cheek,
    the bruises
        on my thighs
            from your grip.

when what I want now
    is beyond proof,
        more than confession
            or memorialization.

    I wear my body like the lake
        wears the shore,

        rubbed at, worn away,
            eroded to a thin blue.

    I wake in what the archive can't contain,
    sleep in the mattress imprint
        of your body next to mine.
call love what it is—

        a worship of
        the hereafter,

            the bits left over,

scraps,
your laugh,
the sour smell
    of your sweat,

my hands
    against your back,
    searching for an opening.

9

forgive me
    my refusal to celebrate
        your cock
        and how you tore me
        open.

I will not lay the riverbank's bright grasses
    underneath your feet
        to ease the passing
            of what's already over.

I am what you made me,
    every day I tire
        of performance
            and apology.

at least now I know
what happens between a man and woman.

        you kill me
        over and over
            until my body
            is a ruin.

10

I overdose on oxycontin,
eight small white pills.

> slip down
> into total
> numbness.

I wake up the next morning

> still alive,
> still in love with him.

> even my suicide is unrequited.

he texts to ask how I'm doing.
I tell him the truth:

> *lol I'm not great tried to kill myself last night*

he calls me six times in a row.

> I wait two hours
> before calling him back.

his voice wavers on the line,
furious, terrified.

> he asks
> *is someone with you*

> but doesn't offer
> to be with me.

I hear the noise of cars rush past
through the phone's speaker.

no I'm alone I just don't want to live like this
anymore

streetcars rumble by
his heavy breath.

he keeps saying

I love you tremendously you are a woman you've always been a
woman

please

I practise undressing in front of you, unbutton my jeans
unhook my bra kneel
in the slanted afternoon light, open my mouth,

wait for you.

I ask you not to call me
good girl

it creeps me out.

you tell me

*it's healing though. like yeah daddy, I'm your good girl and I want
to please you*

push your cock into my throat
as far back as possible,
buck your hips.

I imagine

your body a concrete pillar
sunk into a river.

I break around you,
slick over
the roughness
of your pubic hair,

you whisper
good girl
to the rhythm
of your thrusts.
I choke on saliva and cum,
breathe through my nose,
count backwards in my head
until it's over.

I don't feel healed but wonder

what's wrong with me

when will I
be good?

he wore his body like a boy pretending to be a man. rode a red
bicycle down bloor street to meet me. denim jackets, second-
hand clothes he stole from goodwill. we eat cheeseburgers in bad
diners across toronto, fight in public parks and on the subway. I
fall asleep on his shoulder in an airplane en route to vancouver.
his hand rests on my leg as if I am a wild deer, lured close to him
by the scent of salt.

why is love ordinary and cruel?

everything I remember of him could belong to any woman who
fell in love with any man in this city.

loving him made me feel as if I were a part of the world. the riot
of new leaves in may breaking open above us. each cluster of
stars above the danforth, sudden and sharp as if I forgot that light
could travel between galaxies and reach us. winter in kensington
market, thin coats and his broad chest breaking the wind in
front of me. dry heaving when he left me, suicidal emails and the
infinite collapse of my hoping.

of course, it's cliché.

men blame women for feeling hurt by how things end but excuse
themselves for never being brave. I want to crawl through time
and grab him by the shoulders, shake him and shout

look at me

use the words

nothing
something
somewhere else

to float my body
down the river's grey tongue

populate the poem
with images I stole
from my life

a boy bends his arms down
laces his fingers together
lifts me up into a tree
around me
cherry blossoms fall
not beautiful
but ruinous

something moves between
the boy and me
haunting with gardenias
down every pathway

look, there's my mother weeping
over my missing genitals

my father, dead at last
by cancer and old age

my face ages
even as my tits grow bigger
all this nothing
is a creek in my heart
wetness in the inner values

say somewhere else
imagine a robin's beak
pecks apart my skull
miniscule cracks
in everything's filament.

he told me a story
           of his grandmother's farm
           in Jamaica,
       something about goats
           and the way sunlight scolded
                every moment.

          I was too distracted
          by his beauty
          to listen.

            I couldn't buy his love with my body
            though I tried again and again
              to fuck my way to
              liberation.

I want
to be desired

by what's forgotten.

              for him to remember
                my hair falling
                  across his face,

        the wound
            caught in my mouth.

how memory ruptures us
          whole again,
      in pieces
        and too late.

15

I said my name to the nurse
and confirmed my date of birth.

she put a needle in my spine,
then I felt nothing.

when I woke up, I was past something—

he brochure they gave me when I left
didn't tell me what.

almost a year later
I make eye contact with a boy

who once said he just wanted to take care of me,
then didn't.

an ocean roars between his eyes and mine.

I understand the price I paid
for the sweet ache between
my thighs.

I write "post op trans girl" in my dating profiles.

I pretend my body is a body
redeemable.

somewhere someone wants what I have,
but what I have

                    is a handful of lake water,
                    a dead sparrow at dawn.

maybe what I'm past isn't my body
but my future.

16

there's beauty
       in everything that breaks open.

           a robin's egg,
               the sun in summer,
                    a girl beneath a boy,
a tranny
      in a hospital bed.

each wound
      another chance

                    to birth light.

a birth certificate is a poem
the government
writes for you.

I've changed my name
my sex
my gender

still
this fraudulent country calls me
"sir."

18

how many times do I recount
the ways
my body was cut,
peeled apart and sutured
in anesthetized slumber,

for you to hear me?

it didn't make me a woman.
I'll never be so
precious.

I have a mouth
between my legs
that speaks the estuaries
of river and dusk.

I would do it again,
even
with a doctor's disdain.

the bloody mucus between my fingers,
my cries while someone
whispers *faggot*
to an orderly.

surgery wasn't about fixing my sex.

I wanted to make
a gesture,

a tear in the lining of me,
a scar where

day could enter.

19

should I give details?

for months
I lay on my back
watching blood flow from my vagina
like mud from a stream.

each day
        I counted sutures as they dissolved,
        revealing what surgery
        had bought me.

my lover came to visit once.

        my best friend called to say
        it was too much for her.

I went to three emergency waiting rooms
        only to be thrown out at dawn,

called a liar
and a whore.

        shot full of morphine
        and regret,

I almost died
        in a hallway.

I watched my body, drugged on whisky
and oxycontin,

      lie in his bed
      as he described the cis girl
          he fucked the night before,

      stood naked in the shower,
          trembling on legs
              that could not stand without buckling,

and cried into the warmth of water.

      now I perform the pitiful tranny

              eager to say
              what is wanted,

              how well I'm trained.

I write about the girl who can't be loved
              without being
                    murdered.

      no language I have
      can ever show

              what it feels like

                                        to touch
                                        my clit

                              hard and hurt
                              like a marigold stem,

                                        wet as a
                                        sturgeon's
                                        mouth.

          my pleasure,
    a secret language

                    to refuse meaning.

20

a tranny's mouth
is a vulgar hole

delusion's reservoir.

the health clinic's diagnosis

patient presents with
persistent gender dysphoria

pushes my body
toward the horizon
called "woman"

I never get to the peninsula
where the sun touches
the shore

no one closes their arms
around me

says

welcome home

I thought
faith acts on premonition
but since

I walked through the hospital doors
sat on the operating table

I stop waiting
on miracles.

the truth is

        everyone's gender was
          built on my disappearance.

21

a trans girl fills the inner eye of any camera,
excess is her garden.

    I am here,
        blossom in your annex bedroom,
            pond and moonlight.

        you got into photography
            to document your conquests.

                cis girls in sepia tones,
                their bodies draped over furniture,
                  your shadow on their skin.

    I've watch them appear on your Instagram
        like wildflowers in alleyways,
            unlooked for and precarious
                as if they might disappear
                in your camera,
                    never seen again.
    it's my turn
        to be visible,
                no longer the ghost beneath you,
                secret vice made
                flesh.

        you promised to photograph me
        after my surgery,
                witness my becoming
                in celluloid sheets,
                document how
                    I escape definition.

it doesn't feel like I imagined,

        my breasts posed in the dark of your bedroom,
        an empty house,
            your mouth fixed in a careful line,
                a half erection hidden
                    in your jeans.
every click of the camera
        reminds me

    I'm so far away
    from beautiful.

I read an essay by another trans girl.

    she said desire was not looking at the object
    but imagining the looker in relation to the object.

you arrange me,

    your lens like your dick
        finds the right angles
            to get you off,
makes me
    into less than a girl,
        more than a body.

to look is a kind of love.
           it imagines the object in relation
              to the subject.
that relation
        is called *need*,

                but you forget

the camera doesn't see the body,
only the energy around the body.

not the lips, but the gloss of lips.
not the girl, but her taste against the air.
not me naked in your bedroom,
but the moon behind me.

not your fingers on the shutter release,
but the sound of your tongue
against my spine.

once you said I wasn't a woman,
just "asserting the identity of a woman,"

mistaking the body for its image,
the relation for the object,
the aperture for the truth.

when I left you,
the last thing I did
was open your camera,
expose the film

to light.

the heart bends back on itself
into ontologies without English names.

I touch your shoulder

                    with the spine of a book
      ask if we can talk.

             you shake your head
               as if I were your child
                  asking you
                          for candy
      in a grocery store line
                too poor
        to answer with anything
but an unvoiced no.

              the poverty of our youth
                was more than economic.
    I never learned how to love
        without first asking
              how much does it cost?

I stare into the wound
behind your eyes.
      there's a history
      to your hurt
            your body a diaspora
                I can't put my arms around

your mouth an island
              I won't ever visit.

our love is impossible

the optics of our skin
the weight of our fathers.

you learned to not show emotion in public

because white people mark your body as
dangerous
in need of
containment or killing.

I'm sorry
I didn't see you
until I saw the shape of your absence.

I stand empty-handed
in the watching room
before you.

there's nothing to say

except

I love you
I'm here

in this body
meet me
halfway
in the pain

of two lives
we don't have words for.

23

between my legs
my body opens to forever

name me by the softness of your touch

look for a sound that catches
in my throat before
midnight spills around us

two scars cup my labia
wet them to draw out
the ache of birth

speak now or never say my name again

there is a low place inside me
the blue dusk
over your tongue

graceless, I break
under you

say starlight say moon
say I am the night
emptying from your body

here we labour with possibility
I am weary with the hunger
we unmake ourselves with

you will fall apart at dawn

but for a moment
you are whole above me

and nothing needs burning

here I am the deepest pink

the lining of a salmon's belly
a peony crushed underfoot

I flower with tightness
flinch away from the movement
of your body in mine

here the interior of my body
meets the world

this is as deep as you can
touch me
without killing me

when the light finds your eyes in mine

our bodies make their own logic
birth a politic
neither hopeful nor deceitful

not male or female
only animal

this breath I draw through my lips
pulls you into waters

blessed with salt
and the voices of dead women

repeat the words
goldenrod lilac and violet
until my skin is coated in pollen

                              everything becomes empty

                                          first
                                    the field fills
                                    with
                                              my
                                    body

you must cross over me
to reach the other side
of her

                  say now
                  say yes

                        say you were only waiting
                        for me to unfurl a canopy of birches

the promise of my sex
is not in your mouth
wet and rising

but in my laugh

                        the sudden breath carrying
                        the heat
                        of our bodies

we will not say love
knowing enough

of grief
to speak

truer words.

24

weary of holding your heart

        your disappearing
        of me
        meets the Vancouver skyline

    a violent encounter
    we call love.

      I wipe rain from
      my face, feel stubble
      in my upper lip

it feels like I will never be warm again.

      you repeat it will be ok
      over and over
I play along to ease you off my back
keep you from breaking
      my skin open again.

      am I the abuser or the abused
      you the hero or the foil

        or are we neither?
      two bodies
      caught in an intimacy

      that contracts and expands
      like a heart.

    I listen to your breath
    asleep by my arm

question our love
like a wren builds a nest
piece by piece carried
in a thin beak, plucked
from an infinite blue cold.

I wake up in the early morning
stumble outside to smoke
return to our room

jar you awake
by the sound of the door closing.

you cry out "hello"
in a child's voice
and I answer

"don't worry, babe. it's just me."

you are sometimes helpless
and it makes me forget the ways you hurt me.

once you raped me
though we don't use
that hard word

we say "because of our history"
or "what happened in your apartment"

I was new on hormones
my breasts budding

you had me undress
cradle them for you

press them together
then you squeezed them

your eyes wide, hungry
I felt my stomach drop.

I want to defend you
I didn't say "stop"

just whimpered, bit my lip

later you say you liked
crossing my boundaries
then claim

I made you fuck me
and you didn't want me

but I washed the blood away.

the tear inside me
left a scar.

in Vancouver, the rape
is everywhere around us

I press my face into your chest

let you rub my back
imagine a safety
I don't feel.

once you admitted you abuse me
then we never spoke about it again

it's easier
to avoid the memory
when I'm not locked in a room
with you for days.

I'm sorry
I thought the trip would be romantic

and it is
you take me to the ocean
to watch the sunset

with a bottle of whisky tucked
in your value village coat.

you cry by the shoreline
I sit away from you

on the rocks
as light disappears.

you hold my hand
ask me in your voice

"you're cold, aren't you?"
and I am, I'm colder than

lake superior.

you take my picture
look at it

and say "damn, girl"
as if I was beautiful.

I wish you had lifted me up
      in your arms toward

                the darkened sky
                and thrown me into the ocean
                held me under

                    until I escaped you

            called me pineshi
            let me fly

with wings dipped in the rust of
oil tankers

      away from you
      and back to myself.

                you didn't.
you loved me

      and that was worse
      though I won't admit it

      until later.

why is it never enough
to say "I loved you"
and be done with it?

do you remember
sitting with me in a tim hortons?
your hands in mine,

you said I could meet your mother
and visit minneapolis.

I did everything you asked of me

wore makeup
got the surgery
trained my voice
grew breasts
practised sweetness
between your legs.

now all we are
is a poem
I wrote from the ruin
of our bodies.

"Sometimes a body is that which happens to you"

—Billy-Ray Belcourt, "NDN Homopoetics"

there's always sunlight in new orleans

my hands never seem to dry
caught in yours
                    our bodies descend
                    through the ninth ward
                        drunk on gin
                            and daybreak
                                        your laugh
        like a house
        collects and holds
                                    every possible joy.

        you're the first girl
        I've ever kissed
                    with tongue

                        and that slow pressure
                        of your hands between my thighs

                mixes with the sound of a rooster
                        crowing next door.

                    all day, people walk past your front porch
                    and say "hello"

                                    as if we're all familiar

you chain-smoke american spirits
                    wear crop tops that show too much cleavage
                    clear polyurethane heels

here and there
       the city swelters closer
I ask you
           if it's possible
              for a trans girl
                   to ever be loved

you laugh
    blow smoke in my face

        lean in
        to kiss me.

some nights
    we sit in the bathtub together
      smoking, drinking tequila

      my body between
      your legs

      my back against your chest
      wondering if

   this much intimacy
      is safe.

      you pour water
        from a plastic cup

        over my neck, run your hands
          down to cup my breasts

   before kissing
      the curve of my spine.

            this is a loving
            more deliberate
              than I know
            how to handle.

   you make a joke
      about my new vagina

   say "if you still had a dick
   we wouldn't be doing this"

and I pretend to laugh
as if it's funny that I've bled my way here.

later when my mouth lowers
to your clit

you gasp above me
and I wonder if we taste
the same now

haunted by the casual way
you remember the difference between our bodies

how I've come into
this wanting flesh

by force.

after you cum
and fall asleep beside me
your arms hooked around my waist

I slip away
to lie in the living room.

alone in a new orleans night
my head swims
with water.

you take me to climb railcars at dusk
    abandoned beside the mississippi

    there's a row of empty lots
      one dilapidated house
        surrendering to rot
a lone restaurant marks the end of the road
    music plays
      and a woman sings old jazz standards

    her voice bathes the air
    in longing

      we brought beer
       cigarettes
         our empty bodies

   half drunk
you tell me
   the vacant lots
      and the ruined house
        are an old plantation

don't look over there
    too long

   in new orleans
    nothing lets go
      things linger
      and they will follow us home
if you let them

so I don't look
    caught by your eyes
        in the slow turn of nightfall

each singular trace of your arm
    against mine

        your mouth, its incandescent taste
        of flint and ash

we keep watch over the river
    as the restaurant's singer
        breathes out a mediocre cover of "feeling good"

of course
    there's a haunting between us
        the plantation's afterlife fills
           the space behind us

still your hand in mine
    makes another music

and we are
        brief as the air in
           your lungs
    momentarily
        here

I will not pretend
    we can shed histories
        like the city resists
           the pull of hurricanes
              and erosion

imagine your body
      next to mine is a breakwater
          a levee
               against all hurts

to refuse joy
      is the braver act
            the only choice
              girls like us

      have left.

we fucked the same guy
    for two years

    some nights he came from me
       to you
           our bodies overlapping
           through his

   you say
            queer love is fucking your ex's ex

   I'm not convinced
         we can flatten our desires

   into anything as easy to name

     without first killing

        what makes us
        human.

a boy fucks you
    while I wait in the other room
        listening to the slap
            of his body against yours.

    we talked about having a threesome
        but I'm glad we didn't.

                I've seen too much of men
                to let a stranger fuck me
                while you watch.

        the ceiling fan sends
           currents of cigarette smoke
              out the open front door into the street.

                a car passes.
                someone calls out hello
                to the driver.

      you cum
                a shuttered gasp
                that bends the day
                back on itself.

    I don't envy him
        your pleasure.

           afterwards you come into the living room
             take the cigarette from my fingers
                kiss my mouth, still wet
                  with him

ask me what I want to eat for lunch.

we go uptown for oysters
        you walk between him and me
                take turns holding hands.

we follow you
caught in something
        as sudden

                as rain.

new orleans is

      the only place I've ever been
      where time staggers home
      drunk.

        though everywhere I find
        evidence of history's neglect
        and its riotous beauty.

you cup your hands
    around my face

        tilt my eyes toward the sun
        and ask me what I want

    another glass of wine
      more menthol cigarettes
        your tongue inside my vagina.

      every small act
        of rebellion we make
          brings me closer
            to forgetting

we only arrived here
on the backs of
our dead.

      soon
      it will be our turn
        to die
        and be
        a place
        lovers come
        to shake off
        their restless
        histories.

don't think I don't know
that memory and longing
makes tourists of us.

        don't imagine
        I forget the spectacle
            of humidity and place
                and origin
                    and diaspora
                        and genocide
                            haunts us.

    I know my place
      is outside
            this ravenous city

            and you
            are not a body
                to claim as
                admission.

I have been the ticket
      to a foreign land,
            fur bride
                tranny
      enough to know
                all I want

                is someone
                who recalls
      the deepest colour
      of night is the almost blue
            of morning.

the fluorescent blue of your eyeshadow
   coils of nag champa
      in the afternoon sunlight

   an empty jug of water
     by the bed

      houseflies gathered
      above the overflowing garbage bag
         like a wreath of squirming flowers

   your bare leg thrown over mine
     the blush of my labia
        against your outstretched hand

        how heat travels through windows
          wood
            and lace

      evening never comes here
        though it is always just about to happen

    the fourth of july parade
      in the french quarter

  a sea of tourists and locals
    fireworks lit from the levee

      a pile of rocks
        called the end of the world

you flutter in front of me
    riot of red floral prints
        your headscarf trailing
           behind you

each translucent image
    leaves residue on my skin.

when they ask me what I know of joy
                and ruin
    I will not name a city
        but a girl.

34

enough of desire's interrogation
give language
its weary absence
and say nothing.

you and I fell in love
in a distant summer
that won't return.

all the things I've loved
you
my dog
the scent of spring earth

outstrip their nomenclature.

better poets
make art
speak to entire histories
of violence.

I want none of it.

forget spillers
and simpson.

there is no greater theory
than the small wonder
of loving a woman
in a place entirely her own

each touch
each mouthful

a kinder text.

literature has nothing to teach me
I don't already know from your voice.

the night before I leave you

we slow dance
to billie holiday
on your kitchen floor

the flies lay maggots in the garbage bin

we sweep them up
in a frantic rush

the candles burn out
on your bedroom dresser

when night comes
we sleep nested against
the sky

my body
twice broken open
seeded with salt
and rust

grows something new
unnamed

made of gin, your scent and the blessed
weight of want.

we take no photographs
leave no record

no ledger
nor archive
to mark our place

only
two drunk girls
in the street

say nothing of splendour
or histories emerging
from our split tongues

once you said fucking me
felt too intimate
too close to bear

and I agreed
not knowing if I should say *I'm sorry*

or

you're welcome

if life wants something more of us
grander in design
world-breaking in our ontologies

make it
from handfuls of a night sky

new orleans

and mildewed sheets

everything beautiful in us
is already
dying.

"no
language is neutral seared into the spine's unravelling.
here is history too."

—Dionne Brand, *No Language Is Neutral*

37

what of history

or nation?

the text repairs itself
to meaning.

I am supposed to be weeping
in the pages.

instead I live.

high on cocaine
you spend hours between my thighs
    rubbing my labia raw

    I didn't know it could hurt
      and feel good like this
        until I met you

sometimes I orgasm
    then close my legs around your head
      trap you
      demand more of your tongue
      while you
        breathless
        and hungry

struggle to keep pace

    later
    I let you fuck me

not because I want it
but because it's expected of me
    to trade pleasure
    on rations

to sell my pussy back
    manage your erection
      as if it were
      an obligation

sometimes

       coming down on weed
       and exhaustion

    you tell me stories
    of tehran

          your boyhood
          in another country
how the air smelled
   what your mother wore in the morning

   your grandfather, now dead
     teaching you accounting
then revolution
   uprising
   your father imprisoned for years

      until fleeing
      to this snow-covered homeland

   now you wait tables
     do lines of coke
        cut and ordered by a debit card

         fuck a tranny
         four times a week

  this love
  between us has an expiration date

     I like the way
     you wrap your arm around my waist

how you squeeze my hands in yours
 and cradle my head against your chest

the soft ways
 you buy my cunt

I lost my second virginity to you
 though you don't know it

of course
 we couldn't have lingered
 in this exchange
 we stretch it out
 for five months

a trans woman
 isn't worth much

my pussy too tight
 laugh too deep

we make peace with our exiles

your home in two places
 my body forever
 in migration.

39

in montreal again
        first time since surgery

I sit beside you in an anarchist café
        with bad coffee.

                        the second woman
                        I've loved

                        it's an almost surprise
                        each time I want you

                too new to this queer desire
                to understand its rules.

once I said you had to get over
the idea of me.

loving a trans woman
                is more about faith
                than tolerance.

        the ordinary wanting—
        caffeine
        your fingers along my bare arm
        a new pair of jeans
        fried chicken

in all the hours I spent
waiting in a hospital bed
            or slipping into
            an opioid sleep

I never imagined
such common lust

                        to be loved
                        for being difficult.

what am I now?

                        foundation on my cheeks
                        a maxipad in my purse

every ray of light

            pierces me as if
                        I'm still
                        made of glass.

transsexuals die every day
           but no one writes books about it.

                    I should account for the privilege
                    of being a learned tranny.

       yes I have read your theory
       though I prefer the poetics

              I make with my body
                 between my legs,
                       on my knees.

                              which of these sins
                              should I answer for?

       I let my hair grow long
          and forget to shave my face.

                something in my persistence
                   betrays my womanhood,

                              reveals me as pretender.
I don't blame you for looking for a more
coherent misery.

              the only good trannies are already dead,

                    marsha p and miss rivera,
                       may they rest in power until

              someone tweets their photographs,

twice yearly
when the cis perform allyship,
conjure our
digital beauty.

I apologize for not failing enough
to be worth saving,

for being raped
but not

beaten,
for writing another book

instead of disappearing.

41

what is poetry for
if not description?

I am never sure
when I've said enough
or need disclaimers.

imagine if language
failed us

and we spoke in gestures

instead of nouns?

without witness,
my body becomes
a field of crabapples,
split-red sour-sweet rotten.

here is a history
several of them
converge
in my mouth
like dandelion seeds
in April.

a country
claims me
without my consent.

I am a woman
until I'm not.

trans is not an identity

but a grave I rise from.

I indict my countries
for their crimes
first genocide
then apathy
I have no monument
big enough to hold my dead.
every day,
a new name blossoms.
this one shot
outside a bar
this one strangled
in her bed
this one stabbed 40 times
by her lover
this one beaten
by a pack of men

who to memorialize
and who to forget?

string a line of bodies
like a curtain around me,
hide my face
under murderous sky.

there is enough to live by

sometimes so much joy
it strips me bare

lilacs grow beside
the city asphalt
and
my mouth can't open
wide enough to sing
the possibility
still left in me.

I

am sometimes this,
suspected of being that,

derelict by night
abandoned by morning.

I never know when I blaze
or crouch,

when detail matters
or consumes.

I exceed
my language

I am more
than this white page

I craft a lodge here

like a lark nests
on a hydro pole,

precarious
and alien.

please

excuse my beauty.

I am

more or less
a poem,

an ndn,

a woman,

this language,
I break

the world
against.

weary of waiting
on miracles
on horoscopes
and tarot cards
on the chance for love
that never stops visiting
but refuses to live here.

I move past hope
into something fierce
and unyielding.
the graceless room
each solitary night
time spent lost
in redrafting
your voice
and the way

you cared for me.

I know my limit
by the careful way
cis people praise me.
my co-worker tells me
my breasts are bigger now
it's
compliment
and menace.

I want to die
            but I don't.

                                    there's a theory to my life
                                    not written but felt.

                        in my dreams
                            I place my body in your bed
                                    and never wake again.
            stay with me

                            nurse my animal hurt.
let me leave the page
            walk through your front door

                        pick lint from off your shoulder
                            linger in your kitchen
                                    tag you on Insta.

be the ordinary intimacy

I always felt I was.

                        I went to the surgeon
                            thinking he would make you
                                love me
                                            you don't
                                            and never will.
how to live in my failure
            to be a woman

                        walk through rain
                            my hair damp
                            and weightless

be in the world

without imagining
your face?

yes, I admit I lied

    this body
        knows nothing
        I can call
            a home.

Postscript

a question
of the text,

        the title
        and the footnote,[1]

    each toward its end,
        the place where language parts
            from meaning

        to emerge
        at the breakwater

        of what unmakes me.

if I've failed,
through artifice or image,
in conjure and by light,

        let me apologize.

    I only wanted to chase
      the end of day

        to the hem of night
        and sit there
        among the new stars
        in a body of spun grass
          until language
            abandons me

        and I turn back,
        reluctant and confused,
          to life.

---

1. I left every poem untitled to foreclose the possibility of loss, but still something is missing.

GWEN BENAWAY is a trans girl of Anishinaabe and Métis descent. She is the author of three previous collections of poetry—*Ceremonies for the Dead, Passage,* and *Holy Wild,* winner of the 2019 Governor General's Literary Award for Poetry. It was also a finalist for the Trillium Book Award for Poetry, the Lambda Literary Award for Transgender Poetry, and the Publishing Triangle Award for Trans and Gender-Variant Literature, and was longlisted for the Pat Lowther Memorial Award. She is the editor of an anthology of fantasy short stories titled *Maiden Mother and Crone: Fantastical Trans Femmes.* She has been a finalist for the Dayne Ogilvie Prize for LGBTQ Writers from the Writers' Trust of Canada, and her personal essay, "A Body Like A Home," was the Gold Prize Winner for the National Magazine Awards in Personal Journalism. She is also currently writing a new book of creative nonfiction, *trans girl in love. day/break* is her fourth book of poetry. She lives in Toronto, Ontario, and is a Ph.D. student at the University of Toronto in the Women and Gender Studies Institute.

Colophon

Manufactured as the first edition of
day/break
in the spring of 2020 by Book*hug Press

Edited for the press by Shane Rhodes
Copy edited by Stuart Ross
Cover design by Kate Hargreaves
Type by Jay Millar

bookhugpress.ca